Empower Your Sunday

Alex Telman

Published by Alex Telman, 2024.

EMPOWER YOUR SUNDAY

First edition. October 5, 2024.

ISBN: 979-8230082378

Written by Alex Telman.

Table of Contents

Table of Contents

Author's Note

Dear Reader,

Thank you for picking up this book and taking a step toward cultivating your inner strength. In our fast-paced world, it's easy to get caught up in the rush of daily responsibilities and lose sight of our own well-being. I wrote this book out of a deep conviction that each of us possesses the ability to strengthen our resilience and enhance our emotional health, and I believe that dedicating Sundays to this purpose can be profoundly transformative.

As a practitioner in the field of personal development, I've witnessed the incredible changes that can occur when individuals commit to self-reflection and intentional growth. The practices outlined in these chapters are drawn from various sources, including mindfulness, psychology, and my own experiences. They are designed to be accessible, adaptable, and relevant to anyone seeking to foster a deeper connection with themselves.

While I provide guidance and suggestions, I encourage you to adapt these practices to fit your unique journey. Each person's path is different, and what works for one may not resonate with another. The key is to approach this process with curiosity and openness, allowing yourself to explore what feels most nourishing and supportive.

Making Sundays a day of inner strength is not just about the activities you engage in; it's about cultivating a mindset that prioritizes self-care and growth. I invite you to embrace this journey, not just as a weekly ritual, but as an ongoing commitment to yourself and your well-being.

I hope you find inspiration, clarity, and empowerment within these pages. Remember, the journey to inner strength is ongoing, and each Sunday presents a new opportunity to deepen your practice and reinforce your resilience.

Wishing you peace, growth, and strength on your journey,

- *Alex*

Introduction: Embracing Inner Strength

In a world that often feels chaotic and demanding, taking time for self-care and reflection can seem like a luxury rather than a necessity. Yet, cultivating inner strength is essential for navigating life's challenges and maintaining emotional well-being. This book invites you to make Sundays—a day traditionally associated with rest and renewal—a dedicated time for building and reinforcing your inner strength.

Every Sunday offers a unique opportunity to pause, reflect, and reconnect with ourselves. It's a chance to step away from the hustle and bustle of daily life, to recharge, and to cultivate practices that foster resilience and self-awareness. By consciously choosing to invest this time in your personal growth, you set the tone for the week ahead, creating a foundation of strength that supports your mental and emotional health.

In these pages, you will discover various practices and insights designed to help you embrace the transformative power of Sundays. Each chapter will explore different aspects of building inner strength, including mindfulness, gratitude, self-reflection, and self-compassion. These practices are not merely activities to check off a list; they are powerful tools that can reshape your relationship with yourself and the world around you.

As you journey through this book, you will learn to cultivate a deeper understanding of your thoughts and feelings, develop a greater sense of purpose, and foster a compassionate inner dialogue. You will find practical exercises, reflective prompts, and encouraging insights that can help you create a sacred space for growth and healing every Sunday.

Ultimately, this book is about more than just setting aside one day a week; it's about establishing a mindset that prioritizes your well-being. By dedicating Sundays to your inner strength, you are taking a significant step toward living a more balanced, fulfilling life.

Join me in this exploration, and let's make Sundays a transformative day of inner strength together. It's time to reclaim your power, nurture your spirit, and embark on a journey toward a more resilient you.

Chapter 1: Defining Inner Strength

Inner strength is a concept that resonates deeply within each of us, yet its definition can vary from person to person. At its core, inner strength refers to the mental and emotional resilience that enables individuals to face challenges, navigate life's ups and downs, and emerge stronger from adversity. It encompasses qualities such as self-confidence, determination, and the ability to maintain a positive outlook even in difficult circumstances.

What is Inner Strength?

Inner strength can be seen as a combination of several psychological and emotional attributes:

1. Resilience: This is the capacity to recover quickly from difficulties. Resilient individuals view challenges as opportunities for growth rather than insurmountable obstacles. They possess a belief in their ability to bounce back, which is crucial for maintaining mental well-being.

2. Self-Awareness: Understanding one's own thoughts, emotions, and motivations is essential for developing inner strength. Self-aware individuals can identify their triggers, recognize their strengths and weaknesses, and respond to challenges with greater clarity and purpose.

3. Emotional Regulation: This involves managing one's emotions in a healthy way. Those with strong inner strength can process their feelings without being overwhelmed, allowing them to remain calm and focused during stressful situations.

4. Positive Mindset: A belief in oneself and an optimistic outlook can greatly enhance one's inner strength. Positive thinkers tend to approach challenges with hope and determination, believing that they can effect change in their lives.

5. Adaptability: Life is unpredictable, and the ability to adapt to new circumstances is a hallmark of inner strength. Flexible thinkers can adjust their

plans and attitudes in response to changing situations, reducing feelings of helplessness.

The Importance of Resilience and Self-Awareness

Building inner strength is not merely about weathering the storms of life; it is about emerging from them with a deeper understanding of oneself and a renewed sense of purpose. Resilience allows individuals to cope with setbacks and hardships, fostering a sense of control over their lives. Similarly, self-awareness provides the insight needed to make informed choices and navigate relationships effectively.

When we cultivate resilience, we equip ourselves with tools to manage stress and adversity. This includes recognizing our patterns of thought and behavior, understanding how past experiences shape our present, and developing coping strategies that promote well-being. Self-awareness complements this process, enabling us to identify when we are struggling and seek support or make necessary changes.

How Inner Strength Influences Our Daily Lives

Inner strength plays a pivotal role in our daily experiences and interactions. It influences how we approach challenges at work, manage personal relationships, and respond to unexpected events. Here are some ways inner strength manifests in our lives:

- Decision-Making: Strong inner strength fosters confidence in decision-making. When faced with choices, individuals with inner strength weigh their options thoughtfully and trust their instincts, reducing feelings of indecision and anxiety.

- Relationships: Healthy relationships are built on mutual respect, communication, and understanding. Inner strength enables individuals to establish and maintain boundaries, express their needs, and navigate conflicts with empathy.

- Goal Achievement: Setting and pursuing goals is essential for personal growth. Those with inner strength are more likely to set ambitious goals and remain committed to achieving them, even when faced with obstacles.

- Overall Well-Being: Finally, inner strength contributes to mental and emotional health. A strong sense of self can reduce susceptibility to anxiety and depression, fostering a more fulfilling and balanced life.

As we embark on this journey to make Sundays a day of inner strength, it is essential to understand the foundational concept of inner strength itself. Recognizing the components of inner strength—resilience, self-awareness, emotional regulation, a positive mindset, and adaptability—will empower us to create meaningful practices that nourish and enhance our inner resources. In the following chapters, we will explore various strategies to cultivate this inner strength, ultimately transforming our Sundays into a powerful catalyst for personal growth and well-being.

Chapter 2: The Power of Reflection

Reflection is a powerful tool for cultivating inner strength. It involves taking the time to think deeply about our thoughts, emotions, and experiences, allowing us to gain insights that can inform our actions and decisions. In this chapter, we will explore the significance of reflection, various methods to practice it, and how dedicating Sundays to reflection can help foster inner strength.

The Importance of Reflection

1. Self-Discovery: Reflection facilitates self-discovery by encouraging us to delve into our inner world. When we take the time to examine our thoughts and feelings, we uncover our motivations, values, and beliefs. This self-discovery process can lead to greater self-acceptance and authenticity.

2. Learning from Experiences: Life is filled with lessons, but we often overlook them in the hustle and bustle of everyday life. Reflecting on our experiences allows us to extract valuable lessons from both successes and failures, enhancing our ability to navigate future challenges.

3. Clarifying Values and Goals: Regular reflection helps clarify what truly matters to us. By evaluating our priorities and aligning our actions with our core values, we can make more intentional choices that contribute to our overall sense of fulfillment.

4. Emotional Processing: Reflection provides a safe space to process our emotions. By acknowledging and understanding our feelings, we can reduce emotional turmoil and develop healthier coping strategies. This emotional processing is crucial for maintaining mental well-being.

5. Building Resilience: Reflective practices can strengthen resilience by allowing us to assess how we've coped with challenges in the past. Understanding our responses helps us develop more effective strategies for facing future difficulties.

Methods of Reflection

To harness the power of reflection, we can employ various methods that resonate with our personal preferences and lifestyles. Here are some effective techniques:

1. Journaling: Writing in a journal is one of the most accessible forms of reflection. By putting pen to paper, we can express our thoughts and feelings without judgment. Journaling can take many forms—gratitude lists, free writing, or prompts that encourage deeper exploration.

- Prompt Example: "What challenges did I face this week, and how did I respond to them?"

2. Meditation: Meditation encourages mindfulness and present-moment awareness, providing a fertile ground for reflection. By sitting in silence and observing our thoughts, we can gain insights into our emotional landscape and identify patterns in our thinking.

3. Nature Walks: Spending time in nature allows for a natural rhythm of reflection. The tranquility of the outdoors can promote clarity of thought, and engaging with nature can inspire deeper contemplation about our lives and priorities.

4. Creative Expression: Engaging in creative activities, such as painting, music, or dance, can serve as a form of reflection. These activities allow for emotional expression and can reveal insights about our inner selves that may be difficult to articulate verbally.

5. Talk Therapy or Coaching: Engaging in conversation with a therapist or coach provides an external perspective that can facilitate reflection. They can help guide the discussion, prompting us to consider aspects of our lives that we might not have explored on our own.

Making Sundays a Day of Reflection

Sundays can be transformed into a dedicated day for reflection, creating a sacred space for introspection. Here's how to establish this practice:

1. Set Intentions: Begin each Sunday by setting intentions for your reflective practice. Consider what you hope to achieve during this time—whether it's gaining clarity, processing emotions, or setting goals for the week ahead.

2. Create a Comfortable Environment: Designate a quiet, comfortable space for reflection. This could be a cozy corner of your home, a favorite park bench, or even a calming room in a café. Surround yourself with elements that inspire peace and focus.

3. Limit Distractions: To facilitate deeper reflection, minimize distractions. Turn off notifications on your devices, and consider disconnecting from social media for the day. Allow yourself the freedom to engage fully in the process.

4. Engage in Reflection Activities: Choose one or more reflective activities from the methods discussed earlier. You might start with journaling your thoughts, followed by a meditation session, and then take a nature walk to further explore your insights.

5. Reflect on Your Week: As you engage in reflection, consider what you learned throughout the week. What went well? What challenges did you face? How did your experiences align with your values and goals?

6. Integrate Insights: Conclude your reflective practice by summarizing the insights you gained. Consider how you can apply these lessons in the coming week. This integration of insights is essential for personal growth and resilience.

Reflection is a powerful catalyst for cultivating inner strength. By dedicating Sundays to this practice, we create a routine that fosters self-discovery, emotional processing, and personal growth. The insights gained through reflection not only enhance our understanding of ourselves but also empower us to navigate life's challenges with greater resilience and clarity. As we continue our journey to make Sundays a day of inner strength, we will explore additional practices that complement reflection and further enrich our emotional well-being.

Chapter 3: Cultivating Mindfulness

Mindfulness is the practice of being present and fully engaged in the moment without judgment. It involves cultivating an awareness of our thoughts, feelings, bodily sensations, and the surrounding environment. In this chapter, we will delve into the importance of mindfulness, explore practical techniques for incorporating it into our lives, and discuss how dedicating Sundays to mindfulness practices can enhance our inner strength.

The Importance of Mindfulness

1. Present-Moment Awareness: Mindfulness encourages us to focus on the present moment rather than dwelling on the past or worrying about the future. This shift in focus can reduce anxiety and stress, allowing us to experience life more fully.

2. Emotional Regulation: By cultivating mindfulness, we can improve our emotional regulation. Being aware of our feelings as they arise enables us to respond thoughtfully rather than react impulsively. This awareness fosters resilience in the face of challenges.

3. Enhanced Self-Awareness: Mindfulness fosters a deeper connection with ourselves. By observing our thoughts and emotions without judgment, we gain insights into our patterns and behaviors, helping us understand our triggers and responses.

4. Stress Reduction: Numerous studies have demonstrated that mindfulness practices can significantly reduce stress levels. By focusing on the present, we can disengage from the mental chatter that often contributes to feelings of overwhelm.

5. Improved Relationships: Mindfulness enhances our ability to communicate and connect with others. When we practice being present with ourselves, we can be more fully present in our interactions, leading to deeper and more meaningful connections.

Techniques for Practicing Mindfulness

To cultivate mindfulness, we can engage in various practices that suit our preferences and lifestyles. Here are some effective techniques:

1. Mindful Breathing: Focus on your breath as it flows in and out of your body. Notice the sensations of inhalation and exhalation. If your mind wanders, gently guide it back to your breath without judgment.

- Practice: Set aside a few minutes each day to engage in mindful breathing. This can be done at any time, whether seated, standing, or lying down.

2. Body Scan Meditation: This technique involves mentally scanning your body from head to toe, paying attention to any sensations, tensions, or discomforts. This practice promotes awareness of physical sensations and helps release tension.

- Practice: Find a comfortable position and close your eyes. Start at the top of your head and slowly move down through each part of your body, taking note of any feelings you encounter.

3. Mindful Eating: This practice encourages us to savor our food fully. By paying attention to the taste, texture, and aroma of our meals, we can enhance our eating experience and cultivate gratitude.

- Practice: Choose a meal or snack to eat mindfully. Focus on each bite, chewing slowly and noticing the flavors. Avoid distractions such as screens or conversations during this time.

4. Walking Meditation: Engage in mindful walking by concentrating on the sensations of each step—the contact of your feet with the ground, the movement of your legs, and the rhythm of your breath.

- Practice: Take a slow, intentional walk in a quiet space. Allow your surroundings to fade into the background as you focus solely on the experience of walking.

5. Mindful Observation: Choose an object in your environment, such as a flower, a candle, or a piece of art. Observe it closely, noting its colors, shapes, and textures. Allow yourself to become fully absorbed in this observation.

- Practice: Spend a few minutes each day focusing on an object. This practice can be done indoors or outdoors, providing an opportunity to connect with your surroundings.

Making Sundays a Day of Mindfulness

Sundays can be a wonderful opportunity to deepen your mindfulness practice. Here's how to make the most of this day:

1. Create a Mindful Morning Routine: Begin your Sunday with a mindful morning routine. This could involve waking up a bit earlier to meditate, enjoy a quiet cup of tea or coffee, or practice mindful stretching.

2. Set an Intention: As you start your day, set an intention for your mindfulness practice. Consider what you hope to achieve—whether it's greater clarity, relaxation, or a sense of connection with yourself.

3. Incorporate Mindfulness Activities: Choose a variety of mindfulness practices to engage in throughout the day. You might start with mindful breathing in the morning, follow it with a body scan, and enjoy a mindful meal during lunch.

4. Spend Time in Nature: If possible, dedicate part of your Sunday to spending time outdoors. Nature provides a natural backdrop for mindfulness, allowing you to connect with the present moment through the sights, sounds, and sensations of your environment.

5. Reflect on Your Mindfulness Practice: At the end of the day, take some time to reflect on your mindfulness experiences. Consider what you learned about yourself and how you felt during your practices. This reflection can enhance your awareness and commitment to mindfulness.

6. Integrate Mindfulness into Your Week: Conclude your Sunday by considering how to integrate mindfulness into your daily routine. Identify specific moments

during the week when you can pause and practice mindfulness, such as during commutes or while taking breaks.

Cultivating mindfulness is a transformative practice that enhances our inner strength and emotional well-being. By dedicating Sundays to mindfulness, we create a nurturing space for self-discovery, emotional regulation, and deeper connections with ourselves and others. As we continue our journey to make Sundays a day of inner strength, we will explore additional practices that complement mindfulness and further enrich our path to personal growth.

A MEDITATION FOR CULTIVATING Mindfulness:

Begin by finding a comfortable position, whether seated or lying down, allowing your body to relax fully. Close your eyes, and take a deep breath in. As you exhale, let go of any tension, allowing your body to soften and settle. Let your breath guide you into the present moment.

Take a moment to bring your awareness to the breath. Feel the cool air as it enters your body, and the warmth as it leaves. Notice how your chest or abdomen rises and falls gently with each inhale and exhale. There is no need to change your breath—simply observe it, allowing it to flow naturally. If your mind begins to wander, gently guide your attention back to the sensation of your breath, knowing that this is a practice of returning to the present.

Now, bring your awareness to your body. Begin at the top of your head and slowly scan down through each part of your body, from your scalp to your toes. As you move through each area, notice any sensations that arise—whether they are subtle or strong. There is no need to judge or change anything. Simply acknowledge what is there. If you notice tension or discomfort, imagine breathing into that space, allowing it to soften with each exhalation.

Feel the connection of your body to the surface beneath you. Ground yourself in the present moment, knowing that you are fully supported.

Now, expand your awareness to the sounds around you. Without judgment, simply notice the sounds, whether they are close or distant. Allow them to come and go without holding on to any one sound. Each sound is part of the ever-changing present moment.

As you continue to breathe, notice any thoughts or emotions that arise. Just observe them, without judgment. Let them pass by like clouds in the sky. Remember, you are not your thoughts, nor your emotions. You are the observer, simply witnessing the flow of experience.

Take a few moments now to reflect on the intention you want to set for this practice. It might be to cultivate greater awareness, to be more present, or to find a sense of peace. Allow this intention to settle into your heart, carrying it with you as you move forward in your practice.

As we near the end of this meditation, gently bring your focus back to your breath. Feel the rise and fall of your chest or abdomen. Let the breath be your anchor to the present moment. With each inhale, feel a sense of calm. With each exhale, release any remaining tension.

When you're ready, slowly open your eyes and bring your awareness back to the space around you. Carry the sense of mindfulness with you throughout your day. Remember that mindfulness is always available to you—each moment is an opportunity to return to the present, to connect deeply with yourself and the world around you.

May you find peace in the present moment and strength in your practice.

A SELF-PRAYER FOR CULTIVATING Mindfulness:

I honor this moment, the present moment, as a sacred space of peace and possibility.

May I be fully awake to the thoughts, feelings, and sensations that arise within me,

embracing each one with patience and compassion, without judgment or fear.

EMPOWER YOUR SUNDAY

Grant me the awareness to recognize when my mind drifts into the past or the future,

and the wisdom to gently guide it back to the here and now.

May I cultivate clarity, so that I may see with clear eyes,

and respond with kindness rather than react from habit.

Help me to listen deeply to my body, to notice its needs and its whispers of tension,

allowing me to release what no longer serves me.

May I be present with the sensations, with each breath, with each step,

tuning into the rhythm of my life and the world around me.

Guide me in strengthening my emotional resilience,

so I may face each challenge with awareness and grace.

Grant me the courage to respond with love and understanding,

so that I may find peace in my interactions and build deeper connections with others.

Bless me with the gift of self-awareness,

that I may understand my patterns, my triggers, and my responses,

and grow with each experience into a more compassionate version of myself.

As I move through this day, may I remember to pause,

to breathe, to notice, and to truly live in the fullness of each moment.

May mindfulness become my way of being—rooted in the present, free of judgment,

and open to the beauty and wisdom of the world around me.

May this practice nurture my inner strength,

and guide me to a place of peace, balance, and deep connection.

Amen.

Chapter 4: Nurturing Self-Compassion

Self-compassion is the practice of treating ourselves with kindness, understanding, and support during difficult times. It involves recognizing our shared humanity and acknowledging that imperfection is a part of the human experience. In this chapter, we will explore the concept of self-compassion, its significance in building inner strength, and practical ways to incorporate it into our Sunday routines.

The Importance of Self-Compassion

1. Emotional Resilience: Self-compassion fosters emotional resilience by providing us with a buffer against negative self-talk and harsh self-judgment. When we approach ourselves with compassion, we are better equipped to handle life's challenges and setbacks.

2. Reduction of Anxiety and Depression: Research has shown that self-compassion is linked to lower levels of anxiety and depression. By shifting our inner dialogue from criticism to support, we can alleviate feelings of inadequacy and hopelessness.

3. Enhanced Motivation: Contrary to popular belief, self-compassion does not lead to complacency. Instead, it promotes a healthy motivation to improve by encouraging us to learn from our mistakes rather than berate ourselves for them.

4. Stronger Relationships: When we practice self-compassion, we cultivate a sense of empathy and understanding for others. This can lead to more meaningful connections and improved communication, as we become more accepting of both our own and others' imperfections.

5. Increased Self-Awareness: Self-compassion encourages introspection and self-awareness, helping us to recognize our feelings and reactions without judgment. This awareness allows us to make conscious choices rather than reacting impulsively.

Understanding the Components of Self-Compassion

Self-compassion consists of three key components:

1. Self-Kindness: This involves being gentle and understanding with ourselves when we fail or face difficulties, rather than being harshly self-critical. It means recognizing our pain and responding to it with care.

2. Common Humanity: Acknowledging that suffering and personal inadequacy are part of the shared human experience helps us feel connected to others. This recognition allows us to see that we are not alone in our struggles.

3. Mindfulness: Mindfulness is essential to self-compassion, as it helps us maintain an objective perspective on our thoughts and feelings. By observing our experiences without judgment, we can respond with kindness rather than fear or avoidance.

Practical Ways to Foster Self-Compassion

Incorporating self-compassion into our lives, especially on Sundays, can help us build a foundation for inner strength. Here are several practices to consider:

1. Compassionate Self-Talk: Pay attention to your internal dialogue. When you notice self-critical thoughts, pause and reframe them. Replace harsh judgments with compassionate statements, such as, "It's okay to feel this way; I'm doing my best."

- Practice: Spend a few moments each day reflecting on how you speak to yourself. Write down self-critical thoughts and practice reframing them into more compassionate phrases.

2. Self-Compassion Break: When faced with a difficult situation, take a self-compassion break. Acknowledge the pain, recognize that suffering is part of the human experience, and respond with kindness.

- Practice: When feeling overwhelmed, place a hand on your heart and take a few deep breaths. Say to yourself, "This is hard right now. I'm not alone in this, and I will treat myself with kindness."

3. Journaling: Writing about your feelings and experiences can be a powerful way to cultivate self-compassion. Express your thoughts and emotions without judgment, and allow yourself to process your experiences.

- Practice: Dedicate a few minutes each Sunday to journaling. Reflect on moments when you were hard on yourself and explore how you could have approached those situations with more compassion.

4. Compassion Meditation: Engaging in loving-kindness meditation can help foster feelings of compassion for yourself and others. This practice encourages you to send thoughts of kindness and well-wishing toward yourself and those around you.

- Practice: Find a quiet space to sit comfortably. Close your eyes and take a few deep breaths. Silently repeat phrases like, "May I be happy. May I be healthy. May I be at ease." Gradually expand this intention to include loved ones, acquaintances, and even those with whom you have difficulties.

5. Gratitude Practices: Cultivating gratitude can enhance self-compassion by shifting your focus from negative thoughts to positive aspects of your life. Recognizing what you are thankful for can promote feelings of worthiness and self-acceptance.

- Practice: Each Sunday, write down three things you are grateful for. These can be simple moments or experiences that brought you joy. Reflect on how these positives contribute to your sense of self.

Making Sundays a Day of Self-Compassion

Sundays are an ideal time to nurture self-compassion, providing an opportunity to slow down and reflect on the week. Here's how to dedicate this day to self-compassion:

1. Morning Reflection: Begin your Sunday with a moment of reflection. Consider your feelings, your achievements, and any challenges you faced. Acknowledge your efforts and offer yourself kindness for whatever you experienced.

2. Create a Compassion Ritual: Establish a ritual that fosters self-compassion. This could involve lighting a candle, reciting affirmations, or engaging in a creative activity that brings you joy.

3. Limit Self-Criticism: Challenge yourself to notice instances of self-criticism throughout the day. When you catch yourself being critical, consciously redirect your thoughts toward kindness and understanding.

4. Connect with Nature: Spend time outdoors, allowing nature to nurture your sense of well-being. Nature has a way of grounding us and providing perspective, making it easier to cultivate self-compassion.

5. End-of-Day Reflection: Conclude your Sunday with a reflective practice. Consider moments of self-compassion you experienced throughout the day and how they made you feel. Acknowledge the progress you've made in treating yourself with kindness.

Nurturing self-compassion is a transformative practice that can significantly enhance our inner strength and emotional resilience. By dedicating Sundays to self-compassion, we create a nurturing environment where we can learn to treat ourselves with kindness, understand our shared humanity, and cultivate mindfulness. As we continue our journey toward making Sundays a day of inner strength, we will explore additional practices that support our emotional growth and well-being.

A MEDITATION FOR NURTURING Self-Compassion:

Begin by finding a comfortable place where you can sit or lie down undisturbed. Close your eyes and take a deep, soothing breath in. Hold it gently for a moment, and as you exhale, allow your body to release any tension or stress. With each breath, feel your body relax deeper into the present moment.

Take a few more slow, deep breaths, letting the rhythm of your breath calm and center you. With every inhale, imagine drawing in peace and kindness. With each exhale, feel yourself letting go of self-judgment and criticism.

Now, bring your awareness to your heart. Imagine placing your hand gently over your heart, feeling the warmth and comfort of your touch. As you rest your hand there, silently speak to yourself: "I am worthy of love and kindness, just as I am." Repeat this affirmation, letting it settle into your heart with each breath.

Notice any thoughts or feelings that arise as you reflect on this statement. Perhaps there is resistance or doubt. If so, simply observe them without judgment. Recognize that it's okay to have these thoughts—they are part of the human experience. You are not alone in your struggles. Let them come and go, like clouds drifting across the sky.

Now, shift your focus to your inner dialogue. Gently ask yourself, "What would it feel like to speak to myself with kindness, with understanding?" As you reflect on this, imagine replacing any critical or harsh words with compassionate ones. Instead of saying, "I should be better," say, "I am doing my best, and that is enough." Allow these words of compassion to replace any negativity or self-judgment.

As you continue to breathe deeply, bring to mind a recent moment when you were hard on yourself. Recall the emotions you felt in that situation. Without judgment, offer yourself compassion for that moment. See yourself with love and understanding, acknowledging that everyone faces challenges and no one is perfect. Allow the warmth of your compassion to wrap around this part of you that is struggling, offering comfort and care.

Now, expand your compassion to all parts of yourself. Imagine embracing both your strengths and your imperfections with love. Understand that these qualities make you whole. Just as you would offer kindness to a friend, offer that same kindness to yourself. "I am enough. I am worthy of care. I am deserving of compassion."

Take a few moments to breathe in deeply, soaking in the sense of kindness you are offering yourself. Let this feeling grow stronger with each breath. With every inhale, let compassion fill your being, and with every exhale, let go of any remaining self-criticism or doubt.

When you are ready, slowly begin to bring your awareness back to the present moment. Gently wiggle your fingers and toes, feeling the connection to your body. When you feel ready, open your eyes, carrying this sense of self-compassion with you.

Remember that self-compassion is always available to you. Each moment is an opportunity to treat yourself with kindness, to offer yourself the same care you would give to a loved one. May you continue to walk this path with gentle awareness and love for yourself.

As you move through your day, hold the intention of nurturing self-compassion in your heart. You are worthy of kindness, understanding, and love, just as you are.

A SELF-PRAYER FOR NURTURING Self-Compassion:

I come to this moment with an open heart, ready to offer myself the kindness and love I deserve.

May I recognize my inherent worth, just as I am, and treat myself with the same compassion I would offer a dear friend.

In times of struggle, may I remember that it is okay to be imperfect.

I am human, and my challenges do not define me.

I embrace my flaws with understanding, knowing they are part of my journey, and I choose to learn from them with gentle patience.

When self-doubt arises, may I replace harsh words with nurturing thoughts.

May I speak to myself with kindness, encouragement, and care,

and remind myself that I am doing my best in each moment.

Grant me the strength to let go of self-judgment,

and the courage to embrace my vulnerability.

EMPOWER YOUR SUNDAY

May I find peace in knowing that suffering is part of the shared human experience,

and I am not alone in my struggles.

Help me to recognize the beauty of my imperfections,

and to honor all the parts of myself with love and acceptance.

May I be mindful of my needs and respond with tenderness,

treating myself with the same compassion I offer others.

As I continue on my path, may I always return to a place of self-compassion,

letting it guide me through difficult moments and reminding me of my worth.

May I live with the understanding that I am enough, exactly as I am,

and that I am deserving of love, care, and kindness—always.

Amen.

Chapter 5: Cultivating Mindfulness

Mindfulness is the practice of being fully present and engaged in the current moment, free from judgment and distraction. It involves observing our thoughts, feelings, and sensations without getting caught up in them. By cultivating mindfulness, we can develop a deeper awareness of ourselves and our experiences, fostering inner strength and resilience. This chapter will explore the importance of mindfulness, its benefits, and practical ways to integrate mindfulness practices into our Sundays.

The Significance of Mindfulness

1. Enhanced Self-Awareness: Mindfulness encourages us to tune into our thoughts and feelings, helping us become more aware of our internal landscapes. This heightened self-awareness enables us to recognize our emotional patterns and reactions, paving the way for personal growth.

2. Stress Reduction: Numerous studies have demonstrated that mindfulness practices can significantly reduce stress and anxiety. By focusing on the present moment, we can break the cycle of rumination and worry that often exacerbates feelings of overwhelm.

3. Improved Emotional Regulation: Mindfulness allows us to observe our emotions without immediately reacting to them. This non-reactive awareness can help us respond to situations with greater clarity and intention, rather than being driven by our impulses.

4. Increased Resilience: Regular mindfulness practice builds resilience by helping us adapt to challenges with a calmer, more balanced perspective. We learn to navigate difficulties without becoming overwhelmed by them.

5. Enhanced Relationships: Mindfulness fosters empathy and compassion, allowing us to connect more deeply with others. By being fully present in our interactions, we can cultivate healthier and more meaningful relationships.

Understanding Mindfulness

Mindfulness is rooted in ancient contemplative traditions, particularly Buddhism, but has been adapted for modern therapeutic contexts. It encompasses several key principles:

1. Non-Judgment: Mindfulness encourages us to observe our thoughts and feelings without labeling them as good or bad. This non-judgmental stance allows us to accept our experiences without resistance.

2. Acceptance: Accepting our thoughts and feelings as they arise enables us to acknowledge reality without trying to change it. This acceptance helps reduce inner conflict and promotes emotional well-being.

3. Present-Moment Awareness: Mindfulness emphasizes the importance of being present. By focusing on the here and now, we can cultivate a sense of peace and clarity, minimizing distractions from the past or future.

4. Curiosity: Approaching our experiences with curiosity allows us to explore our thoughts and feelings without attachment. This playful inquiry encourages us to discover new insights about ourselves.

Practical Mindfulness Practices

Incorporating mindfulness into our Sundays can enhance our overall sense of inner strength. Here are several practices to consider:

1. Mindful Breathing: Taking a few moments to focus on your breath is a simple yet powerful way to cultivate mindfulness. Notice the sensations of your breath as it enters and leaves your body.

- Practice: Find a quiet space to sit comfortably. Close your eyes and take a deep breath in through your nose, feeling your chest and abdomen expand. Exhale slowly through your mouth, letting go of any tension. Repeat this for five minutes, gently bringing your focus back to your breath whenever your mind wanders.

2. Body Scan Meditation: This practice involves bringing awareness to different parts of your body, promoting relaxation and a deeper connection to your physical self.

- Practice: Lie down in a comfortable position and close your eyes. Begin by taking a few deep breaths, then bring your attention to your toes. Notice any sensations, tension, or relaxation in that area, and gradually move your focus up through your body—feet, legs, torso, arms, and head—spending a few moments on each area.

3. Mindful Walking: Walking mindfully allows you to engage with your surroundings while also fostering a sense of grounding.

- Practice: Take a leisurely walk in a quiet environment. Pay attention to the sensations of your feet touching the ground, the movement of your legs, and the rhythm of your breath. Observe the sights, sounds, and smells around you, fully immersing yourself in the experience.

4. Mindful Eating: This practice encourages you to savor your food and pay attention to the experience of eating.

- Practice: Choose a small meal or snack. Before eating, take a moment to appreciate the colors, textures, and aromas. As you eat, chew slowly, and notice the flavors and sensations. This mindful approach can enhance your appreciation for food and foster a deeper connection to your body.

5. Journaling for Mindfulness: Journaling can serve as a mindfulness practice by allowing you to reflect on your thoughts and feelings without judgment.

- Practice: Set aside time on Sunday to journal about your experiences from the past week. Write freely, allowing your thoughts to flow onto the page. Focus on how you felt in various situations and any insights you gained. This process can help clarify your emotions and cultivate mindfulness.

Making Sundays a Day of Mindfulness

Sundays are a perfect opportunity to dedicate time to mindfulness practices that cultivate inner strength. Here's how to create a mindful Sunday routine:

EMPOWER YOUR SUNDAY

1. Morning Mindfulness Ritual: Begin your Sunday with a mindfulness practice. This could be a short meditation, mindful breathing, or gentle yoga. Set an intention for the day, focusing on the quality of presence you wish to cultivate.

2. Digital Detox: Consider unplugging from technology for part of your Sunday. This break allows you to be more present and engaged with your surroundings and helps reduce distractions.

3. Engage in Mindful Activities: Throughout your Sunday, choose activities that promote mindfulness. Whether it's gardening, cooking, or spending time in nature, engage fully in the experience.

4. Reflect on Your Day: At the end of Sunday, take time to reflect on how mindfulness influenced your day. Consider moments when you felt present and engaged, as well as any challenges you faced in staying mindful.

5. Set Intentions for the Week Ahead: As you prepare for the upcoming week, set intentions based on your mindfulness experiences. Consider how you can incorporate mindfulness practices into your daily routine.

Cultivating mindfulness is a powerful way to enhance our inner strength and emotional resilience. By dedicating Sundays to mindfulness practices, we can foster a deeper connection with ourselves and the world around us. As we continue our journey toward making Sundays a day of inner strength, we will explore additional practices that support our emotional growth and well-being. Mindfulness not only helps us navigate life's challenges with grace but also enriches our experiences, allowing us to fully appreciate the beauty of the present moment.

A MEDITATION FOR CULTIVATING Mindfulness:

Find a quiet and comfortable space where you can sit or lie down. Gently close your eyes and take a deep, calming breath in. Allow your lungs to fill with air, and then slowly exhale, letting go of any tension you may be holding in your body. With each breath, feel yourself becoming more relaxed, more present.

Begin to notice the rhythm of your breath, without changing it. Simply observe. Feel the sensation of the air entering your nostrils, the rise of your chest, and the gentle release as you exhale. Let your attention rest on the breath—this simple act of breathing.

As you breathe, let go of any thoughts that may be occupying your mind. If thoughts arise, acknowledge them without judgment, and gently return your focus to your breath. You do not need to engage with these thoughts, only to notice them and let them drift away, like leaves floating on a river.

Shift your awareness now to your body. Notice the sensations where your body meets the ground, the chair, or wherever you are sitting or lying. Feel the weight of your body being supported by the earth beneath you. Notice the way your muscles feel—are they tense or relaxed? Take a moment to observe the physical sensations in your body without labeling them as good or bad. Simply acknowledge them, accepting whatever is present.

Now, gently guide your attention to your thoughts and emotions. Notice what is happening in your mind right now. Are there any worries, judgments, or distractions? Acknowledge them without resistance, as if you were a kind observer, simply noticing what is there. You do not need to follow these thoughts or become involved in them. Let them come and go as they please, like clouds drifting across the sky.

Bring your awareness back to the present moment. Feel the sensation of your breath once again. Take a slow, deep breath in, and as you exhale, feel yourself letting go of any lingering tension. With each breath, you are grounding yourself further into the here and now. This moment is all there is.

Imagine now, with each breath you take, you are cultivating a space of peace and presence within you. You are creating a stillness that is always available, no matter the chaos or noise around you. Let this sense of calm fill you, like light pouring into a room. Allow it to settle into your heart and mind.

If your mind wanders, that's okay. Gently return your attention to your breath, to your body, to the present moment. There is no need to rush, no need to perfect your practice. Simply be here, in this moment, observing, accepting, and allowing.

Take a few more deep breaths. As you inhale, imagine you are breathing in calm and clarity. As you exhale, release any tension or distraction. Allow your breath to anchor you firmly in the now, in this moment of mindfulness.

When you feel ready, gently begin to bring your awareness back to your surroundings. Wiggle your fingers and toes, feeling the connection to your body and the earth beneath you. Slowly open your eyes, carrying with you the calm and presence of this practice.

As you move through your day, carry the sense of mindfulness with you. Remember, the present moment is always here, available to you, waiting for you to return to it. Whenever you feel distracted or overwhelmed, return to your breath, to your body, to the present. It is always your anchor, your strength, your point of peace.

May you continue to cultivate mindfulness, allowing it to guide you through the ups and downs of life, offering clarity, peace, and resilience in every moment.

A SELF-PRAYER FOR CULTIVATING Mindfulness:

Divine presence within me,

I come to you in this moment, seeking peace and clarity.

Help me to remember the sacredness of the present moment.

Guide me to release distractions and gently turn my attention inward.

May I be aware of my breath, of my body, of my thoughts,

Without judgment or resistance, simply observing, simply being.

Teach me to meet each moment with openness and acceptance,

And to embrace whatever arises with kindness and compassion.

Grant me the strength to stay grounded,

Even when my mind wanders or my emotions overwhelm.

May I cultivate the ability to respond with calm,

To face challenges with a balanced and open heart.

Help me to see the beauty in the present,

To notice the small details, the simple truths,

And to cherish the quiet spaces where peace resides.

May mindfulness bring me closer to the depths of my own being,

And guide me to live with greater presence, clarity, and love.

As I walk through this day, may I remain anchored in the now,

And trust that each moment is enough.

With gratitude, I allow myself to be fully here,

Aware, accepting, and at peace.

Amen.

Chapter 6: Embracing Self-Compassion

In our journey toward inner strength, cultivating self-compassion is vital. Self-compassion involves treating ourselves with the same kindness, understanding, and support that we would offer a friend in times of struggle. It acknowledges our imperfections and challenges, allowing us to embrace our humanity without judgment. This chapter explores the significance of self-compassion, its benefits, and practical ways to integrate self-compassion practices into our Sundays.

The Importance of Self-Compassion

1. Understanding Self-Compassion: Self-compassion is rooted in the work of psychologist Kristin Neff, who identifies three key components: self-kindness, common humanity, and mindfulness. Self-kindness involves being gentle and understanding toward ourselves when we experience failure or pain, while common humanity recognizes that suffering is a universal human experience. Mindfulness entails maintaining a balanced awareness of our emotions without over-identifying with them.

2. Reducing Self-Criticism: Many of us have an inner critic that harshly judges our mistakes and shortcomings. Self-compassion acts as a counterbalance to this critical voice, promoting a more nurturing and supportive inner dialogue. By cultivating self-compassion, we can reduce feelings of shame and inadequacy, leading to greater emotional well-being.

3. Enhancing Resilience: Self-compassion fosters resilience by encouraging us to face difficulties with an open heart. Instead of avoiding or suppressing our emotions, self-compassion allows us to acknowledge our struggles and respond to them with care and understanding. This resilience helps us navigate life's challenges with greater ease.

4. Improving Mental Health: Research shows that self-compassion is associated with lower levels of anxiety, depression, and stress. By fostering a compassionate

relationship with ourselves, we create a supportive internal environment that promotes mental health and emotional stability.

5. Building Better Relationships: Self-compassion can enhance our relationships with others. When we are kind to ourselves, we are more likely to extend that kindness to others. This compassionate perspective fosters empathy and connection, improving our interpersonal dynamics.

The Three Components of Self-Compassion

1. Self-Kindness: This component encourages us to treat ourselves with care and concern rather than harsh judgment. Self-kindness involves acknowledging our struggles and comforting ourselves in times of pain.

- Practice: When you experience a setback or feel inadequate, pause and offer yourself words of kindness. Remind yourself that it's okay to struggle and that you're deserving of compassion. For example, you might say, “I'm doing my best, and it's okay to feel this way.”

2. Common Humanity: This aspect emphasizes that suffering is a shared human experience. Recognizing that everyone faces challenges can help us feel less isolated in our pain.

- Practice: Reflect on moments when you felt alone in your struggles. Then, remind yourself that countless others have experienced similar feelings. You might say to yourself, “I'm not alone in this; many people go through difficult times.”

3. Mindfulness: Mindfulness allows us to observe our thoughts and feelings without becoming overwhelmed by them. It involves being aware of our emotions and acknowledging them without judgment.

- Practice: When negative emotions arise, practice mindfulness by taking a step back. Observe your feelings without trying to change them. Acknowledge their presence and remind yourself that it's okay to feel this way.

Practical Self-Compassion Exercises

EMPOWER YOUR SUNDAY

Integrating self-compassion into our Sundays can deepen our emotional resilience. Here are some exercises to practice:

1. Self-Compassion Letter: Write a letter to yourself expressing compassion and understanding regarding a struggle you are currently facing.

- Practice: Set aside time to write this letter. Begin by addressing yourself in a kind tone, acknowledging your feelings, and offering words of encouragement. Focus on expressing kindness and understanding, just as you would to a close friend.

2. Compassionate Visualization: Visualize a compassionate figure, such as a loved one or a wise mentor, who embodies kindness and support. Imagine this figure offering you comfort and understanding.

- Practice: Sit quietly and close your eyes. Picture this compassionate figure sitting beside you, listening to your concerns without judgment. Allow yourself to absorb their kindness and support, feeling your heart open to their compassion.

3. Self-Compassion Break: When you encounter a challenging moment, take a self-compassion break to reconnect with your inner kindness.

- Practice: Pause and take a deep breath. Acknowledge your feelings and remind yourself that it's okay to struggle. Repeat a self-compassion mantra, such as, "I am worthy of love and kindness, even when I'm struggling."

4. Gratitude Reflection: Cultivating gratitude can enhance self-compassion by shifting our focus from criticism to appreciation.

- Practice: At the end of Sunday, reflect on three things you are grateful for, including aspects of yourself. This could be recognizing your resilience, creativity, or the effort you put into overcoming challenges.

5. Compassionate Affirmations: Create a list of positive affirmations that resonate with self-compassion.

- Practice: Write down affirmations such as, "I am enough," "I deserve love and kindness," or "It's okay to make mistakes." Repeat these affirmations throughout your Sunday to reinforce a compassionate mindset.

Making Sundays a Day of Self-Compassion

To make Sundays a day dedicated to self-compassion, consider the following practices:

1. Morning Self-Compassion Ritual: Start your Sunday with a self-compassion ritual. This could include journaling, meditation, or reciting affirmations that foster a compassionate mindset.

2. Digital Detox: Limit your exposure to social media and digital distractions. Use this time to focus on self-reflection and engage in activities that promote self-compassion.

3. Engage in Kind Activities: Spend time doing activities that nurture your spirit, such as reading a favorite book, taking a leisurely walk in nature, or practicing a hobby you love.

4. Compassionate Conversations: Reach out to a friend or loved one and engage in a compassionate conversation. Share your feelings, and offer each other support and understanding.

5. End-of-Day Reflection: Conclude your Sunday with a reflection on the day's experiences. Acknowledge moments when you practiced self-compassion and consider how these practices can continue throughout the week.

Embracing self-compassion is a transformative journey that enhances our emotional well-being and inner strength. By dedicating Sundays to self-compassion practices, we create a nurturing space for healing and growth. As we continue our exploration of making Sundays a day of inner strength, we will delve into additional practices that empower us to cultivate resilience, joy, and fulfillment in our lives. Through self-compassion, we learn to embrace our humanity, fostering a kinder and more supportive relationship with ourselves.

MEDITATION FOR EMBRACING Self-Compassion

Find a comfortable position, sitting or lying down, and allow yourself to relax. Close your eyes and take a deep breath, inhaling slowly and deeply through your nose, then exhaling gently through your mouth. With each breath, feel the tension in your body begin to melt away.

Now, bring your awareness to your heart center, the area around your chest. With each breath, imagine you are breathing in love, kindness, and warmth. As you exhale, release any tension, judgment, or self-criticism you may be holding onto.

Feel the loving energy surrounding your heart. This is your own compassion, the same kind of compassion you would offer a dear friend in times of struggle. Allow this warmth to grow with each breath, gently expanding, filling your entire being with a sense of comfort and understanding.

Now, think of a time when you struggled or felt pain. It could be a recent challenge or an older memory. Notice how your body feels as you recall this moment. Without judgment, acknowledge your pain and allow yourself to feel it fully. Recognize that it is okay to feel this way, that it is part of being human.

Now, imagine speaking to yourself in the kindest, most gentle voice. You might say to yourself:

"It's okay to feel this way. I am here for you. You are doing your best, and that's enough."

Notice how your body responds to these words. Allow the warmth of compassion to fill the space of your heart, embracing the tender parts of yourself that need care and understanding.

Remember, you are not alone in your struggles. Suffering is part of the human experience. Everyone faces challenges, and you share this common humanity. You are not isolated in your pain; you are connected to others who are also navigating the ups and downs of life.

Now, shift your awareness to the present moment. With each breath, bring yourself back to the now. Observe any thoughts or feelings that arise without judgment. Simply allow them to pass, like clouds in the sky. Remind yourself that it's okay to experience these feelings, that you do not need to hold onto them or let them define you.

You are worthy of love and kindness, especially from yourself. As you continue breathing, let this self-compassion flow through you, gently releasing any harshness or criticism. Embrace yourself as you are, with all of your imperfections and strengths. You are enough, just as you are.

Take a few moments in silence, letting this love and compassion settle deeply within your heart. Feel the peace that comes from accepting yourself fully, from offering yourself the same support you would give to a loved one.

As we conclude this meditation, take a deep breath in, feeling the sense of calm and compassion expand within you. Slowly exhale, grounding yourself in the present moment. When you're ready, gently open your eyes, bringing with you the warmth of self-compassion that you can carry into the rest of your day.

Remember, you are always worthy of this compassion, no matter what challenges you face. You are deserving of love and care—starting with yourself.

SELF-PRAYER FOR EMBRACING Self-Compassion

Dear Divine Presence within me,

I come before you with a heart open to receive your love and grace. I ask for your guidance as I embrace the practice of self-compassion, learning to treat myself with the same kindness, understanding, and care that I offer to others.

In moments of struggle, remind me that it is okay to feel pain, to face challenges, and to acknowledge my imperfections. Help me to be gentle with myself, especially when my inner critic rises. May I quiet the voice of judgment and instead hear the voice of love and acceptance within.

Grant me the strength to embrace my humanity, knowing that I am not alone in my suffering. Allow me to remember that pain is part of the human experience, and in that shared experience, I am connected to others. Help me to see my struggles as opportunities for growth, rather than as failures to be ashamed of.

May I learn to forgive myself for my mistakes, to accept my flaws, and to honor the journey I am on. Teach me to speak to myself with the same words of comfort and encouragement that I would offer a beloved friend. May I learn to rest in the knowledge that I am enough, exactly as I am.

Grant me the courage to stand tall in my vulnerability, to allow compassion to flow through me, and to trust that I am deserving of love—especially from myself. May I carry this compassion with me, not just in moments of difficulty, but in every step I take, so that I may walk through life with a heart full of understanding and grace.

May I be gentle with myself today, tomorrow, and always. And may I always remember that I am worthy of the love and care I give so freely to others.

Amen.

Chapter 7: Empowering Mindfulness

As we continue our journey to make Sundays a day of inner strength, we turn our attention to the practice of mindfulness. Mindfulness is the art of being fully present in the moment, without judgment or distraction. It allows us to cultivate awareness of our thoughts, feelings, and surroundings, fostering a deeper connection to ourselves and our experiences. This chapter explores the importance of mindfulness, its benefits, and practical strategies to integrate mindfulness practices into our Sundays.

The Essence of Mindfulness

1. Definition of Mindfulness: Mindfulness is derived from ancient contemplative practices, particularly within Buddhist traditions. It involves paying attention to the present moment with openness and curiosity. Jon Kabat-Zinn, a pioneer in mindfulness research, defines it as "the awareness that arises from paying attention, on purpose, in the present moment, and non-judgmentally."

2. Mindfulness vs. Multitasking: In our fast-paced, multitasking world, we often find ourselves distracted and fragmented. Mindfulness encourages us to slow down and engage fully with whatever we are doing. This shift from multitasking to single-tasking can enhance our productivity and satisfaction in daily activities.

3. The Mind-Body Connection: Mindfulness emphasizes the connection between the mind and body. By tuning into our physical sensations and emotions, we can cultivate a holistic understanding of our experiences. This awareness can lead to better emotional regulation and stress management.

The Benefits of Mindfulness

1. Stress Reduction: Numerous studies have shown that mindfulness can significantly reduce stress. By focusing on the present moment, we can interrupt the cycle of worry and rumination, promoting a sense of calm and relaxation.

2. Improved Focus and Concentration: Mindfulness training enhances our ability to concentrate and focus. When we practice being present, we learn to direct our attention intentionally, leading to greater productivity and effectiveness.

3. Enhanced Emotional Regulation: Mindfulness fosters emotional awareness, allowing us to recognize and process our feelings without becoming overwhelmed. This emotional regulation helps us respond to challenges with clarity and composure.

4. Increased Resilience: Mindfulness cultivates resilience by encouraging us to approach difficulties with curiosity and acceptance. Instead of resisting discomfort, we learn to navigate challenges with a sense of openness and adaptability.

5. Greater Self-Awareness: Engaging in mindfulness practices helps us develop a deeper understanding of our thoughts, emotions, and behaviors. This self-awareness empowers us to make intentional choices that align with our values and aspirations.

Mindfulness Practices for Sundays

To fully embrace mindfulness on Sundays, consider integrating the following practices into your routine:

1. Mindful Morning Ritual: Begin your Sunday with a mindful morning ritual. As you wake up, take a few moments to stretch, breathe deeply, and set an intention for the day. Focus on your breath, noticing the sensations of inhaling and exhaling.

- Practice: Spend 5-10 minutes sitting quietly, focusing on your breath. If your mind wanders, gently guide it back to your breath without judgment. Set a positive intention for your day, such as "I will embrace today with openness."

2. Mindful Eating: Transform your meals into mindful experiences. As you eat, pay attention to the flavors, textures, and aromas of your food. Chew slowly and savor each bite.

- Practice: Choose one meal on Sunday to eat mindfully. Put away distractions, such as your phone or television, and fully immerse yourself in the experience of eating. Notice how this practice enhances your appreciation for food.

3. Nature Walk: Spend time in nature and practice mindful walking. Engage your senses by observing the sights, sounds, and smells around you. Allow yourself to connect with the natural world.

- Practice: Go for a walk in a local park or natural setting. Pay attention to the feeling of the ground beneath your feet, the sounds of birds, and the colors of the environment. If your mind wanders, gently return to your surroundings.

4. Mindfulness Meditation: Dedicate time to mindfulness meditation, focusing on your breath, body sensations, or a specific mantra. This practice can deepen your sense of presence and inner calm.

- Practice: Find a quiet space to sit comfortably. Set a timer for 10-20 minutes and focus on your breath. If thoughts arise, acknowledge them and return your focus to your breath. This practice can be a powerful anchor for your Sunday.

5. Mindful Reflection: At the end of your Sunday, take time to reflect on your experiences. Consider how mindfulness influenced your day and how it felt to be present in each moment.

- Practice: Spend a few minutes journaling about your Sunday. Reflect on moments when you practiced mindfulness, how it affected your mood, and any insights you gained throughout the day.

6. Gratitude Practice: Combine mindfulness with gratitude by acknowledging and appreciating the positive aspects of your day.

- Practice: As you wind down for the evening, list three things you are grateful for. Take a moment to savor the feelings of gratitude and presence as you reflect on these experiences.

Overcoming Challenges in Mindfulness Practice

1. Dealing with Distractions: It's natural for the mind to wander during mindfulness practices. When this happens, gently acknowledge the distraction and return your focus to the present moment.

2. Managing Frustration: If you find it challenging to remain present, be patient with yourself. Mindfulness is a skill that takes practice, and it's normal to experience ups and downs.

3. Creating a Supportive Environment: Set up a comfortable and quiet space for your mindfulness practices. Consider using soft lighting, calming scents, or soothing music to enhance your experience.

4. Consistency Over Perfection: Aim for consistency rather than perfection in your mindfulness practice. Even short moments of mindfulness can have a positive impact on your overall well-being.

Integrating mindfulness into our Sundays provides a powerful opportunity to cultivate inner strength and resilience. By embracing the present moment and developing a deeper awareness of our thoughts and feelings, we enhance our ability to navigate life's challenges with grace and compassion. As we continue to explore ways to make Sundays a day of inner strength, we will discover additional practices that empower us to cultivate a fulfilling and meaningful life. Through mindfulness, we learn to appreciate the richness of each moment, fostering a deeper connection to ourselves and the world around us.

EMPOWERING MINDFULNESS Meditation

Find a comfortable place to sit, where you can relax and be at ease. Close your eyes gently, and begin to bring your attention inward.

Take a deep breath in through your nose, feeling the air fill your lungs. Slowly, exhale through your mouth, releasing any tension or stress. With each breath, allow yourself to settle more deeply into the present moment.

Grounding in the Present Moment:

As you continue to breathe, bring your awareness to the present moment. Notice the sensations in your body — the feeling of your feet on the ground, the warmth of your body, and the stillness around you. With each inhale, feel the air entering your body, filling you with calm. With each exhale, release any distractions, worries, or concerns.

In this moment, you are exactly where you need to be. Allow your body to relax and your mind to become still.

Mindfulness of Breath:

Now, bring your focus to your breath. Notice the gentle rise and fall of your chest or belly with each inhale and exhale. There is no need to control your breath, simply observe it as it is. Feel the coolness of the air as it enters your nostrils, and the warmth as it leaves your body.

If your mind begins to wander, that is okay. Gently guide your focus back to your breath, without judgment. Just notice and return, each time with kindness.

Mindfulness of the Body:

Now, expand your awareness to your body. Starting from the top of your head, slowly scan down through your body. Notice any areas of tension or discomfort. As you breathe, soften into these areas, allowing them to relax.

Feel the weight of your body grounded into the surface you are resting upon. With each breath, feel more connected to your body, more present in this moment.

Mindfulness of Emotions:

Now, turn your attention to your emotions. Without trying to change or judge what you feel, simply observe your emotional state. Are there feelings of calm, joy, or perhaps something more challenging like frustration or sadness?

Whatever is present, allow it to be there. Breathe into it. You are not your emotions, but simply the observer. They are part of the human experience, and they will come and go, like clouds in the sky. Let them flow without attachment.

Mindfulness of the Environment:

Now, gently expand your awareness to your surroundings. If you're sitting outside or in nature, listen to the sounds around you. Notice the sensation of the air, the warmth of the sun, or the coolness of the breeze.

If you're indoors, tune in to the subtle sounds in the environment — the hum of electricity, the rustling of leaves outside a window, the feeling of space around you. There is no need to judge or change anything; simply observe it, as it is.

Gratitude and Presence:

As we conclude this practice, take a moment to bring to mind one thing you are grateful for right now. It could be something simple, like the peace of this moment, the air you breathe, or the awareness you are cultivating.

Feel the gratitude in your heart, and as you do, notice how it transforms your experience of the present. Allow this feeling of gratitude to expand, filling you with warmth and contentment.

Closing:

When you're ready, begin to bring your awareness back to the present moment. Gently wiggle your fingers and toes. Take a few more deep breaths, and when you feel ready, slowly open your eyes, bringing the sense of mindfulness and presence with you as you move forward into the day.

Remember, mindfulness is always available to you. With every breath, you can return to the present moment, cultivating inner peace, clarity, and strength.

EMPOWERING MINDFULNESS Self-Prayer

I come into this moment with gratitude and openness. I am here, now, present with my breath, my body, and my heart. In this stillness, I find strength, peace, and clarity.

May I be fully aware of the beauty that exists in each moment, without judgment or distraction. May I embrace each thought, feeling, and sensation with compassion and understanding, knowing that they are part of the human experience.

I release the need to be perfect and accept myself as I am. I trust in the process of mindfulness, knowing that each moment of awareness brings me closer to my true self. I choose to let go of past regrets and future worries, and I welcome the present with an open heart.

May I cultivate the ability to focus and direct my energy with intention, knowing that through mindfulness, I become empowered. I welcome each challenge and difficulty as an opportunity to grow, to learn, and to expand my capacity for resilience.

As I breathe, I align with the present moment, grounding myself in the here and now. I am at peace with the ebb and flow of life, knowing that I have the power to respond with clarity and calm, no matter what arises.

May I be kind to myself, embracing my imperfections with love and patience. I honor the journey I am on, trusting that every step is bringing me closer to deeper awareness and inner strength.

Today, I affirm that mindfulness will guide me, that presence will empower me, and that I am worthy of peace, joy, and growth. I release the distractions of the world, and I commit to living with intention and awareness.

In this moment, I am whole. I am enough. I am present.

And so it is. Amen.

Chapter 8: Empowering Self-Compassion

In our journey toward making Sundays a day of inner strength, we come to a pivotal practice: self-compassion. Often overlooked in the pursuit of personal growth, self-compassion is a powerful tool for transforming how we respond to ourselves, especially in times of struggle or failure. Rather than simply embracing self-compassion, we can empower it, making it a deliberate practice that strengthens our sense of self-worth and resilience. This chapter explores the significance of self-compassion, its benefits, and practical ways to integrate this transformative practice into our Sundays.

The Essence of Empowering Self-Compassion

1. **Definition of Self-Compassion:** Coined by Dr. Kristin Neff, self-compassion is defined as treating ourselves with kindness, understanding, and acceptance in moments of difficulty. It involves three core components:
    - **Self-Kindness:** Treating ourselves with care and warmth, especially in times of failure or pain, rather than harsh self-criticism.
    - **Common Humanity:** Recognizing that suffering is part of the shared human experience, connecting us to others rather than isolating us.
    - **Mindfulness:** Maintaining a balanced awareness of our painful thoughts and feelings, without over-identifying with them or suppressing them.
2. **Self-Compassion vs. Self-Esteem:** While self-esteem is often based on external validation and comparison to others, empowering self-compassion is rooted in an intrinsic sense of worth. It emphasizes unconditional acceptance of ourselves, regardless of our achievements or shortcomings, providing a more stable foundation for our sense of value.

The Benefits of Empowering Self-Compassion

1. **Enhanced Emotional Resilience:** Empowering self-compassion nurtures emotional resilience, helping us bounce back more effectively from setbacks. It allows us to embrace challenges with courage and understanding, knowing we are worthy of care in difficult times.
2. **Reduced Anxiety and Depression:** Research shows that self-compassion can reduce anxiety and depression by counteracting negative self-talk and self-judgment. When we offer ourselves kindness instead of criticism, we mitigate the impact of negative emotions.
3. **Improved Relationships:** When we practice self-compassion, we not only improve our relationship with ourselves but also enhance our relationships with others. By treating ourselves with compassion, we naturally extend that kindness to those around us, deepening our connections and empathy.
4. **Increased Motivation:** Contrary to the belief that self-criticism is a necessary motivator, empowering self-compassion can be a powerful driver for change. It allows us to take action from a place of love and support, free from the fear of harsh judgment.
5. **Greater Overall Well-Being:** By empowering self-compassion, we cultivate a greater sense of well-being. When we accept ourselves unconditionally, we develop a deeper appreciation for our unique journeys, leading to greater satisfaction and peace.

Cultivating Empowered Self-Compassion on Sundays

To fully empower self-compassion on Sundays, consider integrating the following practices into your routine:

1. **Self-Compassion Break:** Take a moment to pause and acknowledge any difficult emotions or challenges you are facing. Empower your ability to navigate these feelings with compassion and understanding.
    - **Practice:** When you notice a challenging emotion, place a hand over your heart and gently say to yourself, "This is a moment of struggle." Follow it with a compassionate phrase like, "I am worthy of care in this moment" or

"It's okay to feel this way."

2. **Journaling with Empowerment:** Dedicate time to journal about your experiences, focusing on empowering self-compassionate reflections. Explore areas where you typically criticize yourself and reframe those thoughts with kindness and understanding.
    - **Practice:** Write a letter to yourself as if you were comforting a close friend. Acknowledge your struggles, express compassion, and offer encouragement. Use this as a tool to shift your mindset and empower your self-worth.
3. **Mindful Self-Compassion Meditation:** Engage in mindfulness practices that specifically cultivate self-compassion. These meditations are designed to foster kindness toward oneself, strengthening the inner resources needed to face life's challenges.
    - **Practice:** Set aside 10-20 minutes for a self-compassion meditation. Focus on your breath, or use guided meditations that center on sending compassion to yourself. Empower your mind to respond with gentleness and care.
4. **Affirmations of Empowerment:** Create a list of self-compassion affirmations to repeat throughout your day. These positive statements can help you cultivate a compassionate mindset, reinforcing your sense of worth and value.
    - **Practice:** Write affirmations such as, "I am enough," "I am worthy of love and care," or "It's okay to make mistakes." Place these affirmations where you can see them regularly to reinforce your empowered mindset.
5. **Gentle Movement Practices:** Engage in gentle movement, such as yoga or stretching, to honor your body and connect more deeply with your feelings. Through this practice, you empower yourself to care for your physical and emotional well-being.
    - **Practice:** Participate in a gentle yoga session or a mindful walk in nature. Focus on the sensations in your body, honoring both your strengths and limitations. Use this time to empower yourself with compassion and care.
6. **Acts of Kindness to Yourself:** Treat yourself to small acts of kindness, whether it's enjoying a favorite meal, indulging in a hobby, or simply resting. These actions empower you to nurture yourself without guilt or hesitation.

- **Practice:** Plan one activity on Sunday that brings you joy, such as reading a book, taking a warm bath, or engaging in a creative project. Empower yourself to savor the moment and prioritize your well-being.

Overcoming Challenges in Empowering Self-Compassion

1. **Combating Negative Self-Talk:** When negative self-talk arises, challenge these thoughts gently. Empower yourself by replacing self-critical thoughts with affirmations of kindness and care.
2. **Addressing Feelings of Guilt:** Many people experience guilt when prioritizing self-compassion. Remind yourself that taking care of yourself is essential for overall well-being, and it enables you to be more present and supportive to others.
3. **Creating a Supportive Environment:** Surround yourself with influences that reinforce your self-compassion journey. Positive relationships, inspiring resources, and supportive environments empower your growth and healing.
4. **Consistency Over Perfection:** Like any skill, empowering self-compassion requires practice. Focus on being consistent rather than perfect. Allow yourself the grace to grow at your own pace, knowing that each step forward is progress.

Empowering self-compassion on Sundays provides a profound opportunity for healing and personal growth. By treating ourselves with kindness and understanding, we cultivate a solid foundation of inner strength that allows us to navigate life's challenges with greater ease and resilience. As we continue to explore how to make Sundays a day of inner strength, we see that empowering self-compassion is not only a practice but a way of being. It empowers us to honor our true selves, fostering resilience, connection, and a deeper appreciation for the journey of life. Through self-compassion, we unlock our ability to create a nurturing space within ourselves, paving the way for a more fulfilling and empowered existence.

MEDITATION FOR EMPOWERING Self-Compassion

Welcome to this empowering meditation designed to help you cultivate and deepen self-compassion. Find a quiet space where you can sit comfortably, either on a cushion, chair, or the floor, with your spine straight and your hands resting gently in your lap. Close your eyes softly and take a deep breath in, allowing your body to relax with each exhale.

1. Settling into the Present Moment

Take a moment to settle into the present moment. Feel the weight of your body grounding you to the earth beneath. Notice the sensations in your body, the gentle rise and fall of your chest as you breathe. Allow yourself to let go of any distractions or worries, bringing your attention fully to this time of self-care and connection.

2. Awareness of the Breath

Now, gently bring your focus to your breath. Notice the coolness as you inhale, and the warmth as you exhale. Let each breath be an invitation to relax more deeply. With every inhale, imagine that you are breathing in love, kindness, and compassion. With each exhale, release any tension or negativity you may be holding onto.

Inhale deeply, breathing in compassion...

Exhale slowly, releasing judgment...

Inhale, feeling warmth and kindness flow through you...

Exhale, letting go of all self-criticism...

Continue to breathe slowly and deeply, allowing each breath to fill you with peace and compassion.

3. Connecting with the Heart

Now, place your hand gently over your heart. Feel the warmth of your palm against your skin. With each heartbeat, know that you are worthy of love and kindness, just as you are, in this very moment. This hand on your heart symbolizes the compassion you are offering to yourself.

If there are any emotions arising—whether joy, sadness, frustration, or doubt—hold them with loving attention, as if you were holding a dear friend in need. Acknowledge that it's okay to feel however you are feeling. There is no need to judge or fix anything. Simply be present with your experience.

4. Affirmations of Self-Compassion

As you continue to breathe, silently repeat the following affirmations. Let each phrase sink deeply into your heart:

- "I am worthy of love and care, just as I am."
- "I honor my feelings and my journey."
- "It's okay to make mistakes, I learn from them with compassion."
- "I am enough, exactly as I am in this moment."
- "I embrace myself with kindness and understanding."

Repeat these words to yourself, allowing the truth of these affirmations to resonate deeply. Let them empower you to release self-judgment and replace it with loving acceptance.

5. Sending Compassion to Yourself

Now, envision a soft light in the center of your chest, radiating warmth and kindness. This light symbolizes your inner compassion. As you continue to breathe deeply, imagine this light growing stronger, expanding with each breath. Let it fill your heart, your body, and your mind.

With every inhale, feel the warmth of self-compassion growing within you. With every exhale, send this compassion to any part of yourself that feels hurt, tired, or in need of healing. Allow the light to reach every corner of your being, offering kindness and acceptance to yourself.

You may silently say to yourself:

"May I be gentle with myself."

"May I be kind to myself in moments of struggle."

"May I give myself the love and care I deserve."

6. Embracing the Present Moment with Self-Compassion

Now, take a moment to reflect on the present moment. Know that you have the power to approach each moment with self-compassion. Whatever challenges you may face, you have the strength to meet them with kindness toward yourself.

Embrace the knowledge that self-compassion is not a luxury, but a necessity. By empowering self-compassion, you are fostering resilience, growth, and healing. You are honoring your humanity, your journey, and your worth.

7. Closing the Meditation

As you begin to bring your awareness back to the room, take a few more deep breaths. Gently wiggle your fingers and toes, bringing movement back into your body. When you're ready, slowly open your eyes, carrying the sense of empowered self-compassion with you into the rest of your day.

Remember, you are worthy of love, care, and kindness. Allow this practice to empower you to navigate life's challenges with compassion and understanding, both for yourself and others.

Take a moment to smile to yourself, knowing that this practice is an act of profound self-love. You are enough, and you are deserving of all the kindness you give yourself.

EMPOWERING SELF-COMPASSION Prayer

Dear Inner Self,

I come to you with an open heart, seeking the strength to be kind, patient, and loving toward myself. In this moment, I ask for the grace to embrace my humanity with tenderness, acknowledging both my strengths and my imperfections.

Grant me the wisdom to treat myself with the same compassion I would offer a dear friend in times of struggle. Help me to release self-judgment and embrace my own worth, knowing that I am deserving of love, care, and acceptance—no matter what challenges I face.

When self-doubt or negativity arise, remind me to be gentle with myself. May I learn to forgive my mistakes and view them as opportunities for growth, not as failures. May I stand strong in the knowledge that I am enough, just as I am, in this very moment.

Guide me to honor my emotions without judgment, to nurture myself with kindness, and to care for my well-being with intentional love. May I find peace in the quiet moments of reflection, and may my heart be open to receiving the compassion I so freely give to others.

I trust in the power of self-compassion to heal, to strengthen, and to empower me. With each breath, I choose to embrace myself fully—without fear, without doubt, and with unconditional love.

Thank you for the gift of self-compassion, for the healing it brings, and for the strength it creates within me. May I carry this compassion within me, sharing it with the world as I walk my path with grace and authenticity.

Amen.

Chapter 9: Practical Tools for Cultivating Inner Strength on Sundays

In this chapter, we will explore practical tools and resources that can empower you to make Sundays a dedicated day for cultivating inner strength. These tools will include meditation scripts, journaling prompts, and checklists that can easily fit into your Sunday routine. By incorporating these practices, you can create a meaningful ritual that enhances your emotional well-being and sets a positive tone for the week ahead.

1. Meditation Scripts

Meditation is a powerful tool for cultivating inner strength. Here are two simple meditation scripts you can use on Sundays:

A. Morning Mindfulness Meditation (10 minutes)

Purpose: To ground yourself and set intentions for the day.

Instructions:

1. Find a quiet and comfortable space where you won't be disturbed.

2. Sit in a comfortable position with your back straight and hands resting on your knees or lap.

3. Close your eyes and take a few deep breaths, inhaling deeply through your nose and exhaling slowly through your mouth.

4. As you breathe, bring your attention to your body. Notice any areas of tension or discomfort.

5. With each exhale, visualize releasing that tension. Feel your body becoming lighter and more relaxed.

6. After a few minutes of focusing on your breath, begin to set your intentions for the day. You might say to yourself:

- "Today, I choose to embrace inner strength."

- "I am capable of overcoming challenges."

- "I am deserving of peace and happiness."

7. Spend a few moments visualizing how you will carry this intention throughout your day.

8. When you're ready, gently open your eyes and take a moment to notice how you feel before moving on with your day.

B. Evening Reflection Meditation (10 minutes)

Purpose: To reflect on the day and cultivate gratitude.

Instructions:

1. Find a quiet space to sit or lie down comfortably.

2. Close your eyes and take a few deep breaths, allowing your body to relax.

3. Bring to mind three things you are grateful for from the day. They can be as simple as a kind word from a friend or the beauty of nature.

4. Spend a few moments savoring each of these experiences. Feel the warmth of gratitude filling your heart.

5. Now, reflect on any challenges you faced. Instead of judging yourself, acknowledge them as opportunities for growth.

6. As you breathe deeply, visualize letting go of any negative emotions tied to these challenges, allowing them to drift away with each exhale.

7. When you feel ready, take a few more deep breaths and gently open your eyes.

2. Journaling Prompts

Journaling is an excellent way to explore your thoughts and feelings. Here are some prompts specifically designed for your Sunday reflections:

A. Weekly Reflection Prompts

1. What did I learn about myself this week?

2. What challenges did I face, and how did I respond?

3. What am I proud of achieving this week?

4. What can I let go of from the past week to create space for new opportunities?

5. How can I nurture my inner strength moving forward?

B. Intention Setting Prompts

1. What are three intentions I want to set for the upcoming week?

2. What steps can I take to honor these intentions?

3. How can I practice self-care in the coming week?

4. What positive affirmations will support me this week?

5. What is one thing I can do each day to cultivate my inner strength?

3. Checklists for Sunday Rituals

Creating a structured checklist can help you stay focused and ensure that you dedicate time to your inner strength practices. Here's a sample checklist for your Sunday routine:

A. Sunday Inner Strength Ritual Checklist

1. Morning Mindfulness Meditation: 10 minutes

2. Journaling Session: Reflect on the past week and set intentions for the upcoming week.

3. Physical Activity: Engage in a form of movement that you enjoy (e.g., walking, yoga, dancing).

4. Self-Care Activity: Dedicate time to a self-care practice (e.g., reading, bathing, or enjoying a hobby).

5. Gratitude Reflection: Write down three things you're grateful for.

6. Evening Reflection Meditation: 10 minutes to reflect on the day.

7. Plan for the Week Ahead: Review your schedule and set priorities.

Integrating these practical tools into your Sunday routine can create a powerful framework for cultivating inner strength. By dedicating time to meditation, journaling, and self-care, you not only enhance your emotional well-being but also establish a nurturing practice that resonates throughout the week. As you commit to these rituals, you'll find yourself becoming more resilient and empowered, ready to face whatever challenges come your way.

SAMPLE MEDITATION SCRIPT 1: Cultivating Inner Strength on Sundays

Purpose: To enhance emotional well-being and set a powerful, focused tone for the day ahead, cultivating inner strength.

Begin by finding a quiet and comfortable space where you won't be disturbed. You may sit or lie down in a position where you can remain relaxed and alert.

Introduction:

Take a deep breath in... and slowly exhale... Allow your body to relax into the ground or chair beneath you. Let go of any tension you may be holding.

As you continue to breathe, feel the weight of your body settle, grounding you to this moment.

Body Awareness:

Now, bring your attention to your body. With each inhale, notice how your body gently rises. With each exhale, feel it soften into the present moment. Scan your body slowly from the top of your head down to your toes.

If you notice any areas of tension, simply acknowledge them and, with your next breath, release that tension. Let it melt away with each exhale, allowing yourself to soften deeper into the stillness.

Breathing and Grounding:

Now, focus on your breath. Inhale slowly and deeply through your nose... and exhale gently through your mouth. Let each breath carry you deeper into relaxation.

Feel yourself becoming more grounded with every breath. Imagine roots growing deep into the earth beneath you, connecting you to the infinite strength and support of the world around you.

Setting Your Intention for the Day:

As you continue breathing, bring your focus to your inner self, your inner strength. Today, you are choosing to be grounded, resilient, and calm. You are embracing your ability to handle whatever comes your way.

Silently or aloud, set your intention for today. Some examples might be:

- "I am grounded in my strength and calm."
- "I embrace this day with openness and courage."
- "I am capable of meeting any challenge with grace."

Let these words sink deeply into your being, knowing that this intention is a part of you. You are fully capable, worthy, and strong.

Visualizing Your Inner Strength:

Now, envision a light within you—a warm, glowing light in the center of your chest. See it growing brighter, radiating outward, filling every part of your being. This light represents your inner strength, your resilience, and your peace.

Allow this light to expand throughout your entire body, embracing you with a sense of warmth, empowerment, and peace. Know that this strength is always within you, ready to be called upon whenever needed.

Affirming Your Strength:

In this peaceful space, gently repeat to yourself the following affirmations:

- "I am strong."
- "I trust in my ability to handle what comes."
- "I am worthy of love, peace, and all that I need."
- "I carry my inner strength with me, always."

Feel the truth of these words resonate deep within you.

Ending the Meditation:

Now, take a few moments to simply breathe, soaking in the peace, strength, and light you've cultivated. When you're ready, gently bring your awareness back to the space around you.

Wiggle your fingers and toes, take a deep breath in... and exhale, opening your eyes when you're ready. Carry the calm and strength from this practice with you throughout your day.

Remember, you have the inner strength to navigate any situation, and it is always with you.

SAMPLE MEDITATION SCRIPT 2: Empowering Your Inner Strength

Purpose: To cultivate a deep sense of inner strength and resilience, grounding yourself in the present moment as you prepare to embrace the day ahead.

Begin by finding a comfortable position, either sitting or lying down. Ensure you're in a quiet space where you can remain undisturbed for the duration of this meditation.

Introduction:

Take a deep breath in... and slowly exhale, allowing yourself to settle into this moment. Let go of any distractions or worries. Allow your body to feel supported by the earth beneath you.

With each breath, you become more present, more centered in your own body, and more aware of the quiet strength within you.

Body Relaxation:

As you continue to breathe deeply, begin to bring awareness to your body. Start with your feet, noticing any sensations. With each breath, allow your feet to relax and release any tension.

Move up to your legs, your hips, and your lower back. Feel the areas soften and loosen with every breath you take.

Now bring awareness to your chest, your arms, and your neck. Feel the weight of your body and the comfort of your breath filling these areas with relaxation and peace.

Lastly, bring your focus to your head, your face, and your jaw. With each exhale, release any tension you may be holding, allowing your entire body to soften.

Connecting with Inner Strength:

Take a deep breath in, and as you exhale, bring your attention to the center of your chest, near your heart. Imagine a powerful, radiant light glowing there—your inner strength.

This light is steady, unwavering, and full of potential. It is a reflection of your courage, resilience, and wisdom. Feel this light grow with every breath you take, expanding and filling your chest with warmth and confidence.

As you breathe in, feel this light growing stronger, and as you breathe out, feel it extending beyond your body, surrounding you with a protective, empowering aura.

Affirming Your Inner Strength:

Now, gently repeat the following affirmations to yourself, either silently or aloud. As you say each one, allow it to resonate deeply within your being:

- "I am strong and capable."
- "I trust in my ability to overcome challenges."
- "I embrace each moment with courage and confidence."
- "I am resilient and face each day with inner strength."
- "I honor my personal power and choose to live with intention."

With each affirmation, feel the truth of these words grounding you, reinforcing your innate strength.

Embodying Strength in Action:

Visualize yourself moving through the day ahead. See yourself walking with confidence, handling challenges with calmness, and making decisions from a place of clarity and power.

Imagine any obstacles or challenges that may arise. Rather than feeling overwhelmed, you meet them with the confidence of knowing that your inner strength is always available to you. You handle each moment with grace, patience, and resilience.

Feel this empowerment filling your entire being, knowing that you have all you need within you to succeed and thrive.

Closing the Meditation:

Take a moment to simply breathe deeply, bringing your awareness back to the room. Feel your body grounded and connected to the earth. Take a few more deep, calming breaths, and when you're ready, gently open your eyes.

Carry the sense of inner strength and empowerment with you as you move forward in your day. Remember, you have everything within you to navigate life with resilience, clarity, and peace.

End of Meditation.

EMPOWER YOUR SUNDAY

This meditation serves to reinforce your inner strength, helping you feel empowered and capable of facing the day with confidence. You can return to this practice whenever you need to ground yourself or strengthen your sense of personal power.

Chapter 10: Challenges and Overcoming Obstacles

As you embark on the journey of making Sundays a dedicated day of inner strength, it's important to acknowledge that challenges may arise. Life can be unpredictable, and the path to personal growth often comes with hurdles. This chapter will explore common obstacles you may encounter and offer practical strategies to overcome them, ensuring that your commitment to inner strength remains steadfast.

1. Time Constraints

Challenge: One of the most common obstacles people face is finding enough time in their busy schedules to dedicate to their inner strength practices on Sundays. Life's demands can easily encroach upon the time you set aside for self-care and reflection.

Strategy: Prioritize and Schedule

- Set Clear Boundaries: Treat your inner strength time as a non-negotiable appointment. Block out specific hours in your calendar dedicated to your rituals and protect that time from distractions.

- Break It Down: If you find it hard to dedicate a large chunk of time, break your practices into smaller, manageable segments throughout the day. For instance, spend 5 minutes meditating in the morning and another 5 minutes journaling in the evening.

- Combine Activities: Look for ways to integrate your inner strength practices into other activities. For example, listen to a mindfulness podcast during your commute or do a short meditation while waiting for your coffee.

2. Lack of Motivation

Challenge: On some Sundays, you may feel a lack of motivation to engage in your inner strength practices. This can be due to fatigue, feelings of overwhelm, or simply not feeling "up to it."

Strategy: Cultivate Accountability and Reward

- Find a Buddy: Share your intentions with a friend or family member and invite them to join you in your Sunday practices. Having someone else involved can motivate you to stay committed.

- Set Rewards: Create a reward system for completing your rituals. Treat yourself to a favorite snack or a leisurely activity after you've completed your inner strength practices. This can help create positive associations with your routine.

- Remember Your "Why": Reflect on the reasons you started this journey. Write down your motivations and keep them visible as a reminder of the benefits you seek to cultivate.

3. Distractions and Interruptions

Challenge: Distractions from technology, household chores, or family members can hinder your ability to focus on your inner strength rituals.

Strategy: Create a Conducive Environment

- Designate a Sacred Space: Set up a specific area in your home for your practices. This could be a cozy corner with cushions, candles, or inspiring quotes. Having a dedicated space can help you associate it with relaxation and focus.

- Limit Technology Use: Consider implementing a "tech-free" time during your rituals. Turn off notifications, silence your phone, and create a barrier between yourself and the digital distractions that may pull you away from your practices.

- Communicate Your Needs: Let family members know about your Sunday rituals. Share the importance of this time for you and ask for their support in minimizing interruptions.

4. Self-Criticism

Challenge: Many people struggle with self-criticism, feeling that they are not doing their practices "correctly" or that they're not making enough progress. This can lead to discouragement and a sense of failure.

Strategy: Practice Self-Compassion

- Acknowledge Your Efforts: Remind yourself that any effort you make toward inner strength is a step in the right direction. Celebrate small victories and recognize that progress takes time.

- Challenge Negative Thoughts: When you notice self-critical thoughts arising, pause and reframe them. Instead of thinking, "I didn't meditate long enough," consider, "I took time to connect with myself, and that's what matters."

- Embrace Imperfection: Understand that there is no "perfect" way to practice inner strength. Allow yourself to be imperfect and embrace the journey with all its ups and downs.

5. Resistance to Change

Challenge: Change can be uncomfortable, and you may find yourself resisting the very practices that could help you grow. This resistance can manifest as procrastination, avoidance, or a desire to revert to old habits.

Strategy: Ease into Change

- Start Small: If you're feeling resistant, begin with brief, simple practices. For example, instead of committing to a full meditation session, start with just a few deep breaths. Gradually increase the duration as you become more comfortable.

- Create a Routine: Establishing a consistent Sunday routine can help reduce resistance over time. When practices become habitual, they require less mental effort to engage in.

- Reflect on Resistance: Take time to explore the source of your resistance. Journaling about your feelings can provide insights into underlying fears or beliefs that may be holding you back.

Making Sundays a day of inner strength is a rewarding journey that may not always be smooth. By recognizing and addressing common challenges, you empower yourself to stay committed to your practices. Remember, it's not about perfection; it's about progress and creating a nurturing space for personal growth. With determination, self-compassion, and practical strategies, you can overcome obstacles and fully embrace the transformative power of your Sunday rituals. As you continue on this path, you will find greater resilience and strength to face the week ahead, reinforcing the commitment you've made to yourself.

MEDITATION FOR OVERCOMING Challenges and Embracing Inner Strength

Purpose: To help you cultivate resilience and navigate obstacles by grounding yourself in inner strength and self-compassion, while fostering a sense of calm and focus.

Find a comfortable position, either sitting or lying down. Ensure you are in a quiet and peaceful space, free from distractions. Allow your body to relax into the surface beneath you.

Introduction:

Take a deep breath in, filling your lungs with fresh, calming air, and exhale slowly, letting go of any tension or stress. With each inhale, you bring in peace. With each exhale, you release any worries or distractions.

Let your body sink deeper into relaxation with every breath, becoming more present in this moment. You are safe, and you are ready to begin this meditation with an open mind and a compassionate heart.

Body Awareness and Relaxation:

Now, gently bring your attention to your body. Begin by noticing the points where your body connects with the surface beneath you. Feel the support, the grounding energy that is always there for you.

Starting at the top of your head, begin to scan your body slowly, noticing any tension or tightness. As you breathe, soften and release any areas that feel tense. Relax your forehead, soften your eyes, relax your jaw, and allow your shoulders to melt away from your ears.

Let your arms and legs relax deeply, and feel a wave of calm move through your entire body, from head to toe.

With each breath, feel more grounded, more present, and ready to embrace the strength within.

Recognizing Obstacles:

Now, bring to mind any challenges or obstacles you may be facing in your life or in your journey toward cultivating inner strength. These could be external distractions, time constraints, or any resistance you may feel toward change.

See these challenges as they are, without judgment, simply acknowledging their presence. Understand that challenges are a natural part of life, and they do not define you or your path. They are simply opportunities for growth.

As you breathe, allow yourself to accept that obstacles are temporary, and within you lies the ability to overcome them.

Connecting with Your Inner Strength:

Take a deep breath in and, as you exhale, bring your attention to the center of your chest, your heart center. Imagine a glowing light of strength and resilience within you. This light represents your inner strength—steadfast, powerful, and unyielding.

With each breath, feel this light grow brighter and stronger. See it expanding, filling your chest with warmth and confidence, until it radiates outward, surrounding you with a protective aura of calm and determination.

Know that this light is always within you. You have the power to overcome any challenge that comes your way.

Affirming Resilience:

Now, repeat the following affirmations silently or aloud, allowing each word to settle deeply within your heart:

- "I am resilient, and I can overcome any challenge."
- "I trust in my ability to handle obstacles with grace and strength."
- "I honor my inner strength and embrace challenges as opportunities for growth."
- "I am capable of making space for what truly matters in my life."
- "I move forward with compassion for myself, no matter the challenges I face."

With each affirmation, feel your confidence and inner power grow. Know that no obstacle is insurmountable when you trust in your strength.

Releasing Resistance:

If you feel resistance or discomfort toward change or self-compassion, allow yourself to acknowledge it with kindness. Know that resistance is a natural part of transformation and growth.

As you breathe deeply, release any resistance with each exhale, allowing yourself to relax into change, knowing that it is a necessary part of your journey.

Imagine the resistance gently fading away, replaced by a sense of ease and acceptance. You are ready to take small steps forward, embracing each moment with compassion for yourself.

Visualizing Your Path Forward:

Now, visualize yourself moving through the upcoming week. See yourself embracing challenges with a sense of inner calm, strength, and clarity.

Imagine yourself handling time constraints with ease, finding moments to practice self-care and strength. See yourself motivated and energized, moving past distractions and maintaining focus on what truly matters.

Picture yourself gently overcoming resistance, moving with grace and patience, and embracing change as part of your growth.

Feel a deep sense of peace and empowerment as you visualize yourself handling each moment with confidence and strength.

Closing the Meditation:

Take a moment to simply breathe deeply, filling your lungs with fresh air, and exhale slowly, feeling gratitude for the strength within you.

Know that no matter the challenges you face, you have the power to overcome them. You are resilient, capable, and strong.

As you slowly begin to bring your awareness back to the room, carry this sense of empowerment and inner strength with you. You are ready to face whatever comes your way with a calm and determined heart.

When you're ready, gently open your eyes, and feel a sense of peace, resilience, and strength as you move forward.

End of Meditation.

This meditation is a powerful tool to help you stay grounded in your inner strength and overcome obstacles with grace and confidence. You can return to this practice whenever you need to reconnect with your resilience and remember your ability to navigate challenges.

Conclusion: A New Beginning Every Sunday

As we draw this journey to a close, we reflect on the transformative power of dedicating Sundays to inner strength. Each chapter has offered insights and practices designed to help us cultivate resilience, self-awareness, and compassion. By embracing these principles, we can create a sanctuary of peace and growth that nourishes our spirit and supports our mental well-being.

The practices we've explored—mindfulness, gratitude, self-reflection, and self-compassion—are not merely activities to fill our time; they are powerful tools for reshaping our relationship with ourselves and the world around us. By setting aside this intentional time each week, we not only honor our own needs but also create a rhythm that reinforces our commitment to personal growth.

A Journey, Not a Destination

It's essential to recognize that this journey is ongoing. Each Sunday offers a new opportunity to reconnect with our inner selves, to assess our emotional landscape, and to cultivate a sense of strength that can carry us through the week ahead. Just as we nurture our physical health, we must also prioritize our emotional and mental well-being.

As we move forward, remember that self-discovery and personal growth are not linear paths. There will be ups and downs, moments of clarity, and times of uncertainty. Embrace this ebb and flow, knowing that each experience contributes to the tapestry of your life. Allow yourself the grace to stumble and the courage to rise again.

Creating a Community of Strength

In addition to individual practices, consider how you can share these principles with others. Whether through informal conversations, group gatherings, or community workshops, fostering a culture of inner strength can amplify the impact of these practices. Supporting one another in this journey not only deepens our connections but also enhances our collective resilience.

A Call to Action

As you embark on this new chapter of making Sundays a day of inner strength, challenge yourself to remain open and curious. Experiment with the practices that resonate most with you, adapt them to your unique needs, and be gentle with yourself as you explore what works best.

Finally, remember that the goal is not perfection, but progress. Celebrate the small victories, acknowledge your efforts, and allow yourself to grow at your own pace. By committing to this journey, you are not just enhancing your own life; you are inspiring others to do the same.

With each Sunday dedicated to nurturing your inner strength, you pave the way for a more fulfilled and resilient life. Embrace the power of this sacred time, and let it be a source of renewal, insight, and joy. The journey begins anew each week, inviting you to step into the fullness of who you are and who you can become.

SELF-PRAYER FOR OVERCOMING Obstacles and Cultivating Inner Strength

Dear Inner Self,

I come before you with an open heart, seeking the strength to overcome the obstacles in my path. I acknowledge the challenges I face, knowing that they are a part of my journey. I ask for the courage to face them, the wisdom to learn from them, and the resilience to rise above them.

Grant me the ability to remain grounded in my inner strength, even when the world feels overwhelming. Help me to stay calm and centered when time is tight, when distractions arise, or when motivation seems distant. Remind me that I am capable of handling whatever comes my way, and that every small step I take toward growth is valuable.

When resistance to change arises, may I find the patience and compassion to move forward gently, without judgment or self-criticism. Let me embrace imperfection with kindness, knowing that I do not need to be perfect to be worthy or strong.

EMPOWER YOUR SUNDAY

Fill me with the confidence to trust in my ability to adapt and to see obstacles as opportunities for growth. May I always find peace in the process, even when the outcome is unclear.

In times of struggle, may I be gentle with myself, offering kindness and understanding, remembering that I am not alone. Help me to always return to my inner light, knowing it will guide me through every challenge and lead me toward a life of strength, peace, and growth.

Amen.

About Alex Telman

ALEX TELMAN IS A GLOBALLY recognized spiritual healer, author, and one of the country's most read poets. With over 45 years of experience, he has dedicated his life to helping individuals break free from negative energies, trauma, and spiritual blockages. His transformative work has empowered a diverse range of clients, including celebrities, business leaders, educators, and everyday individuals, guiding them toward emotional well-being, personal growth, and spiritual fulfillment.

From an early age, Alex demonstrated extraordinary abilities to perceive and remove harmful energies and entities, a gift that first emerged when he was just three years old. This rare talent led him to study with psychic masters across the globe—Afghanistan, France, Sweden, Israel, England, and Australia—each recognizing his unique gifts and helping him refine his craft.

In addition to his healing practice, Alex has practiced as a barrister, teacher, university lecturer, and small business owner, offering a well-rounded perspective on healing that combines spirituality with practical action. He is also an accomplished author, whose writings inspire and uplift readers by exploring the depths of human emotion and the power of self-healing.

Through his sessions, Alex has helped countless individuals overcome emotional turmoil and reclaim their lives. His work transcends cultural and geographical boundaries, offering profound healing to those in need. His mission is simple yet powerful: to guide people back to their authentic selves, helping them live with purpose, peace, and fulfillment.

With a career built on compassion, wisdom, and deep spiritual insight, Alex remains a beacon of hope for anyone seeking to overcome their struggles and wanting to step into a life of clarity and joy.

Other Titles by Alex Telman

Non Fiction

Think Like a Modern Guru

Mastering Hypnosis: Complete Step-by-Step Manual, Case Studies, and Sample Scripts

From Cursed to Cured: 100 True Stories of Healing from Curses

Connecting to the Afterlife: a how-to guide

Your Journey from Death to Rebirth

Empower Your Sundays: Unlocking Inner Strength for a Resilient Life

The Truth Behind the Creation Story: A Journey Through Reincarnation

Practical Mentalism in a Nutshell

Reprogram Your Mind in a Nutshell

Meditation in a Nutshell

Alex Telman in Quotes

Novels

The Loom of Fate

A Happy Death

One Life, Half Lived

Down and Out in Byron Bay

God Speaks: A Journey Through Creation in His Own Words

Jesus Speaks: The Man Behind the Miracle in His Own Words

Poetry

Telman: The Complete Haiku 1974-2024

Echoes of September 11

Homeless in New York

Burning Echoes of Time

From Dawn to Dusk: the life cycle in sonnets

Eternal Echoes: The Tapestry of Time and the Unseen

Snapshots of People I Have Never Met

Legends and Lessons: 36 Myths Unveiled

A Measure of Time: The Eternal Voyage of Self

Ashes of Verses: Poems Burned But Not Forgotten

Reflections on Solitude: A Poetic Journey Through The Lonely Mind

Your Friendship is a Museum

Whispers to Bella

ACKNOWLEDGEMENT FOR cover photo: Maria Mari Nutriciolog-via Pexels

Don't miss out!

Visit the website below and you can sign up to receive emails whenever Alex Telman publishes a new book. There's no charge and no obligation.

https://books2read.com/r/B-A-YBSCC-TMPBF

BOOKS 2 READ

Connecting independent readers to independent writers.

www.ingramcontent.com/pod-product-compliance
Lightning Source LLC
LaVergne TN
LVHW010458160826
845677LV00012B/2548